Beautiful Parks
For Kids

Nature Books for Kids
By K. Bennett
Mendon Cottage Books

JD-Biz Publishing

I0439624

Purchase at Amazon.com

Download Free Books!
http://MendonCottageBooks.com

Table of Contents

Introduction

*Earth and sky, woods and fields, lakes and rivers, the mountain and the sea, are excellent schoolmasters, and teach some of us more than we can ever learn from books. ~ **John Lubbock***

***

Parks are wonderful places to spend time with friends and family. They can be big and green with lots of trees, flowers, and water. Some parks have water and marine animals that do fun tricks. Hiking trails are also found in parks, and places to camp out at night.

Parks are everywhere and have different names like: National parks, public or recreation parks, marine parks, water parks, and amusements parks. This type of park might be your favorite!

Do you know what makes each park different? Find out the answer to this question in chapter 1.

The First Parks

Many years ago, the United States made the first National Park in 1872. That year, 3,400 square miles was set aside to make the Yellowstone National Park, and this park is still very famous today.

And in 1879, Australia made the world's second National Park. Since that date, lots of other parks were made all over the world.

DID YOU KNOW?

One of the biggest and most beautiful hot springs is found in Yellowstone National Park. Every 60 seconds, it bubbles up gallons of hot, hot water into the air. This hot spring is called: The Grand Prismatic Spring.

The spring has bright rainbow colors that might seem fake, but it is real! Do you know how the spring gets so colorful? It's because of small microscopic bacteria that live in the boiling waters. How hot does the water get? Over 180 degrees Fahrenheit!

Yellowstone National Park is not the only amazing park we can learn about. There are many more places to discover. Would you like to learn what makes each park unique?

Then join me on this quest to explore the wonderful world of …

Beautiful Parks!

Chapter 1: Types of Parks

In the beginning, we learned about many different types of parks. Let's see what makes each one so special and interesting.

National Parks: National parks are big, beautiful spaces with lots of interesting animals, trees, and flowers. They usually belong to the government or the town, and many people visit them all year long.

Some famous National Parks around the world are: Yosemite National Park, Victoria Falls National Park, Everglades National Park, Rocky National Park, Grand Canyon National Park, Hawaii Volcanoes National Park, and many more! In chapter 2 we will find out what makes each one of these parks so amazing.

If you love fun activities, there are lots of wonderful things to do at parks. Think about these great ideas:

-Hiking

-Bicycle riding

-Camping

-Horseback riding

-Climbing

-Bird watching

-Picnicing

-Painting

-Fishing

-Taking pictures

-Water sports… and lots more.

Which park do you like best, and what fun thing would you like to do there?

<u>Recreation Parks:</u> This kind of park is full of fun activities. These parks are for the public so everyone can enjoy them. Some are not very big but it is still a nice place to visit.

There are neat things to do at recreation parks like: play playground games, ball games, or just enjoy the wide outdoors. Can you think of other ideas?

-Ride a bicycle through a field of flowers and smell the sweet perfume.

-Walk on a nice trail and see where it takes you.

-Enjoy a nice, tasty picnic.

-Fly a kite and watch it soar!

-Role play with your friends. Use the playground equipment to have fun. Decide which object is a castle, a dragon, a horse, or a knight in shining armor.

-Play hide and seek, tag, or tug of war.

-Hide something in the park and go on a treasure hunt.

-If there is a pond, find and feed the ducks. See if any baby ducks were born and feed them too.

-Spot a rainbow and count the colors. Draw a picture of what you see and share it with your friends and family. Don't forget to have fun.

This list is just some ideas. Come up with some good ones on your own!

Marine Parks: Marine parks are natural places to protect sea creatures in their home. The park acts like a preserve to keep the habitat of animals safe. The word "preserve" simply means to hold or keep something. So the marine park works hard to keep the animals safe and protected.

One of the largest Marine parks in the world is the Great Barrier Reef of Australia. In Jamaica, we find the Montego Bay Marine Park. And in Malaysia, the Turtle Islands Marine Park is full of green turtles and Hawksbill turtles that lay their eggs in the sand.

 Marine parks have lots of fun activities to explore like:

-Swimming and snorkeling.

-Studying different types of corals.

-Learning about many kinds of fishes, sea creatures, and sea birds.

-Riding in a glass bottom boat or an underwater submarine.

Is this something you would like to do? Then ask your parent or a guardian if you can visit a marine park near your home.

<u>Water Parks:</u> Water parks are amusements parks with lots and lots of water! At a water park you will find water slides, spray grounds, swimming, bathing, splash pads, and much more.

One of the biggest water parks in the world is called Water World in Denver, Colorado. Aquaventure is another big park in the Caribbean. This park is full of slides, mountains, rafting rides, and water playgrounds.

If you are in the Caribbean or near the coast and you don't like any of these activities, you might like to swim in the beautiful waters and enjoy the warm tropical sun.

Amusement Parks: This kind of park is very different from the other parks. It full of colorful and exciting things to do all the time! An amusement park is a place with shows, restaurants, games, mechanical rides, and activities for any age group.

Can you guess which park is the most famous park in the world? Did you guess Walt Disney World? That's right! This type of park is also known as a theme park. Other amusement parks are Six Flags and Busch Gardens.

There are many fun rides at amusement parks like the carousel, roller coasters, train rides, Ferris wheels, bumper cars, fireworks, and water slides.

Did you have any fun experiences the last time you visited an amusement park? If you have never been there, ask your parent or a guardian to take you. I am sure you will have a great time!

Chapter 2: National Parks

 Now that you've learned about the different types of parks, let's talk about what makes them so special and exciting.

Yosemite National Park: This amazing park is called: "A jewel of wild spaces." It is full of giant sequoia trees and that live for a very long time. Do you remember these trees? We talked about them in our book on "*Beautiful Trees*."

"***Sequoia Trees:*** These trees are the "Kings" of trees. They are not only very big but also very wide. They are called "nature's skyscrapers" because they grow high into the sky. If you were to stand below one of these amazing trees, you will feel very small.

We can find lots of old Sequoia trees at Yosemite National Park. Some of them have lived to be more than 3,000 years old! That's an old, old, tree.

What else can we find?

Yosemite Valley has one of the biggest granite monoliths in the world called **El Capitan**. You may not know what a monolith is, so let's explain. **Dictionary.com** says a monolith is something formed by a single block of stone.

This is what happened at the park. It took years and years and years of rivers and glaciers to make interesting rock formations. The rock is granite and this material is hard, strong, and lasts for a very long time.

There are other interesting rock formations at the park called Cathedral rocks, Half dome, Sentinel rock, and Glacier point.

Mule deer, chipmunks, marmots, pikas, and the brush rabbit all live in Yosemite. And a beautiful waterfall called Bridal Veil Falls flows some months of the year.

There are lots of neat things to do at Yosemite and here are some of them:

-See a ranger show.

-Ride your bicycle in Yosemite Valley.

-Have fun at the nature center of Happy Isles. This place is made for children with lots of fun things to do.

-Find out about the Junior Ranger program.

-Visit the Yosemite museum.

-Visit the gardens and learn about the local natives.

Yosemite National Park is a great destination to learn more about the beautiful nature around us.

**Victoria Falls**: This beautiful park is between Zimbabwe and Zambia, and has the largest waterfall in the world. zCan you guess how high this waterfall is?

1- **120**

2- **354**

3- **200**

4- **100**

The correct number is...2! It is approximately 354 feet high and 1 mile wide. This waterfall is also called Mosi-oa-Tunya in the native language, which means: "smoke that thunders."

Elephants and hippos live around these beautiful falls and when the rainy months come, more than 540 million cubic meters of water flows over the top every minute. Does that sound like a lot? That is because it is!

These falls are not too easy to explore. Some people use helicopters to look at them from in the air. Other people walk along the trails and swim in the falls. But it is not safe and can be dangerous to get too close to the edge. Can you guess why? That's right! You might fall off and it is a long, long, drop!

DID YOU KNOW?

The falls are named after Queen Victoria. A missionary and explorer from Scotland by the name of David Livingston traveled to the falls and named it after the Queen in November, 1855.

__Everglades National Park:__ This park is big place with over 1 million acres. The park has different habitats with lots of wildlife.

The word habitat means a place where animals live. They also use it to store food, and other resources they may need. There are many different habitats in the World, like swamps, mountains, trees, oceans, and deserts, to name a few.

There are five habitats in the Everglades with interesting names like Mangrove, Pineland, Hammock, Slough, and Sawgrass. Lots of animals live there too! You can find alligators, tree frogs, American crocodile, otters, manatees, and more. Because of its great diversity, many people visit the Everglades every year.

__Rocky National Park:__ The Rocky National Park is full of amazing trees and tall mountains. Lots of trails lead to interesting places where you can see lots of wildlife along the way. People love to ride the trails on horses and there are lots of fun nature trails and lake trails.

The Moraine Park Museum has interactive exhibits that kids will love, and the ranger program is another fun activity at the park. If you love wildlife and animals, you will enjoy the large number or Elk in the area. You might even see bighorn sheep snacking on tasty mud pies. Yes, they eat mud, they think that it tastes delicious!

The trail ridge road is another exciting attraction at the park. Many families love to eat picnics or enjoy the wildlife in the area. There are also hiking trails with great views of the sky, the clouds, and the mountains.

**Grand Canyon National Park:** The Grand Canyon National Park is a wonderful place with beautiful things to see and do! Many people call it a "wonder of the natural world." It is like taking a space ship back in time millions of years ago. Here are some fun things to enjoy at the park.

The Rim Trail: This is a nice place for everyone in the family. The trail is big enough to walk on and it has beautiful stones with lots of benches to stop and rest.

The Yavapai Observation Tower: This tower has a table with puzzle pieces on it. It's a great place to see the beautiful sights of the Canyon and have fun playing with puzzles!

Mule Rides: Have you ever ridden a mule before? This is a great time to try. The rides go around the Bright Angel Trail to Plateau Point and the Indian Garden. Not all riders are permitted. You have to be at least 4 feet 7 inches high and weigh less than 200 pounds. The spots fill up fast so the earlier you call the better! Sounds like fun… don't you agree?

Hawaii National Park: This park is a special kind of park because it's a volcano park! There are over 300,000 acres in this park and it is full of lots of exciting things. This park can be dangerous so it is important to make plans before you decide to visit. Why?

Fog and ash from the volcano may be in the air. This can cause breathing problems and may not be safe for everyone. It is important to keep this in mind if you want to visit.

Here are two amazing things to do at the Volcano Park:

Thurston Lava Tube: This lava tube or tunnel is a neat formation and a great place to explore. Around the tube you will find trees and leaves that look like something from the dinosaur age.

Do you remember how lava tubes are formed? In our book on "*Beautiful Caves*" we explained how it works.

"When a Volcano erupts and tube of Lava flows down a hill. When it cools down and gets really hard, the inside of the Lava tube is hollow and this is where a Cave forms."

These tubes look very interesting but I don't know if I want to explore one...how about you?

Jagger Museum: The Kīlauea Caldera can be seen from this museum and it glows red in the dark. There are interesting geological exhibits and rocks at the museum with different types of lava. You can even touch the rocks and see what it feels like. There is also scientific equipment on display to measure powerful volcanoes and information on Hawaii's culture and history.

Chapter 3: Fun facts!

I hope you are enjoying this book on Beautiful Parks around the world! Here are a few more neat facts you may like to know about:

- Parks are full of high and beautiful mountains. If you hike up mountain trails, do you remember why you need to be careful not to climb too high? In our books on "*Beautiful Mountains*" we explained the reasons why: "If you get too high, the oxygen can be too low and you will not have enough air to breathe. This is called a "death zone" and it is approximately 23,000 to 26,000 feet high. If you wandered into this part of the mountain, you could only be there for a few minutes before you lose consciousness. To stay so high, you would need to have oxygen tanks or bottles to breathe."

-The Grand Canyon is called one of the "Seven natural wonders of the world." This canyon has some of the oldest rock formations on planet earth. Scientists say that it is over 1 billion years old! And the limestone rock is around 230 million years old. How many more years do you have to live to get that old? Use a calculator to find the number!

- The Junior ranger program is something many kids love to do and the programs are usually free to join. A Junior park ranger gets free booklets with lots of puzzles and learning activities to protect the park and the wild animals. Is this something you would like to do?

-Hot Springs National Park in Arkansas is the the smallest national park in the United States. It is around 5,500 acres in size but the biggest National Park is Wrangell - St. Elias National Park in Alaska. It is over 8 million acres! What is the biggest park that you know about?

-In the Yellowstone National Park we find the Yellowstone Caldera. This is a super volcano that scientist think will blow its top 100,000 years in the future!

- Sometimes people get confused with National Parks and National Monuments. Do you know what makes them different?

 - A National Park is known for neat geological formations, natural beauty, and strange ecosystems. A National Monument is chosen for its archaeological and historical importance.

Parks are great to explore! I hope you have learned more about what makes each one so special.

Vocabulary: Here is a small list of vocabulary words to help you learn more about the wonderful world of parks.

- -Geomorphological
- -Giant sequoia
- -John Muir
- -Ridge
- -Slope
- -Geology
- -Ledge
- -Conservationist
- -Unexplored
- -Terrain
- -Natural resource
- -Acclimatization
- -Canyon walk
- -Biosphere
- -Thermal
- -Ecosystem
- -Ecological
- -Naturalist
- -Erode
- -Dissolve
- -Flora
- -Geology
- -Panorama

Do you know what these words mean? If you are not sure, ask your parent or a guardian's permission to search for the definition online.

Don't forget to get permission before you search.

(*www.dictionary.com*)

Conclusion:

***In conclusion*:**

The idea of a national park started many years ago by a painter named George Caitlin. When he saw the natural wonders around him he wanted to keep them safe and protected.

Today, many people feel the same way and they work hard to keep the parks beautiful. National Parks and other parks are full of life and make the world around us a fun place to live.

Most of the parks are full of mountains, which offer protection to animals and people. The parks are also fun to explore.

Another idea

There are tons of fun activities you can do at the parks. This can be biking, walking, exploring, picnicing, bird watching, hiking, and even river rafting.

Which activity do you like best?

What else can you do?

Do you live near a park or would you like to visit one of them? Why don't you ask your parents or your guardian to take you there? You can look up the location online and see what kind of park it is. Then you could use a map and a notebook to explore.

If you do not like the idea visiting a park or if it too hard to get there, why don't you learn more about the wildlife that lives there?

Another choice

If you decide to explore a park you might see strange trees or beautiful flowers you have never seen before. Why don't you take a picture and try to find out more about it? You could even use it for show and tell at school. Or you might decide to share it with friends and family. Whatever choice you make, have fun!

One more idea!

The wildlife in the park or the trees and flowers are great choices for science experiments. If you decide to use this subject don't forget the steps you need to make it a great project.

Steps:

1 – You need to ask a **question** to be answered by observation or experimentation. Make it a very interesting question so your classmates and teachers will want to learn the answers!

For example: What kind of wildlife can you find at the park? Does it live in the mountain or in the lake? How big or small is it? What does it look like?

2 – The next step is to state a **Hypothesis**. This is a big word but Sciencekidsathome.com explains it like this*: It is a tentative explanation for an observation, phenomenon, or scientific problem that can be tested by further investigation.*

Sounds complicated? Think of it like this: Your hypothesis is what you think the results of your project will be when your research is all done!

3 – Next on the list is: **Procedure.** This is very important. Procedure will help you discover the answer to your question and prove what you are trying to say.

There are other experiments online that can help you. Ask your parent or a guardian to help you search. Or ask for permission before you search.

4 – **Results**. You will need to show your results and all the information you collected for your project.

5 – **Conclusion**. Finish up with what you learned and then answer the question you had in Step 1. If you can't answer the question, explain why the question cannot be answered.

If you don't like the ideas in this book, brainstorm your own ideas and come up with your own conclusions. I am sure you will do an amazing job. We hope you have enjoyed this book on Beautiful Parks. And remember…

"Educating the mind without educating the heart is no education at all." - *Aristotle*

Happy Learning!

Sources:

http://www.skwirk.com/

http://easyscienceforkids.com/all-about-victoria-falls/

http://www.travelforkids.com/Funtodo/Arizona/Grand_Canyon/grand-canyon-village.htm

http://www.sciencekids.co.nz/sciencefacts/earth/grandcanyon.html

https://www.vocabulary.com/lists/122348#view=notes

https://www.dosomething.org/us/facts/11-facts-about-national-parks

https://kidskonnect.com/fun/amusement-parks/

Author Bio

K. Bennett loves to write for both children and adults. Many subjects are interesting to research, but writing for children is special to her heart.

Her favorite pastimes include reading, traveling and discovering new things. Each of these activities helps to fuel her imagination and acts like a blank canvas waiting for more stories.

She is intrigued with fantasy elements like hidden worlds and faraway lands. And basically anything that gets her imagination soaring to new heights!

Her writing credits include children books online, short stories for online magazines, and novellas listed at Amazon.com

Download Free Books!

http://MendonCottageBooks.com

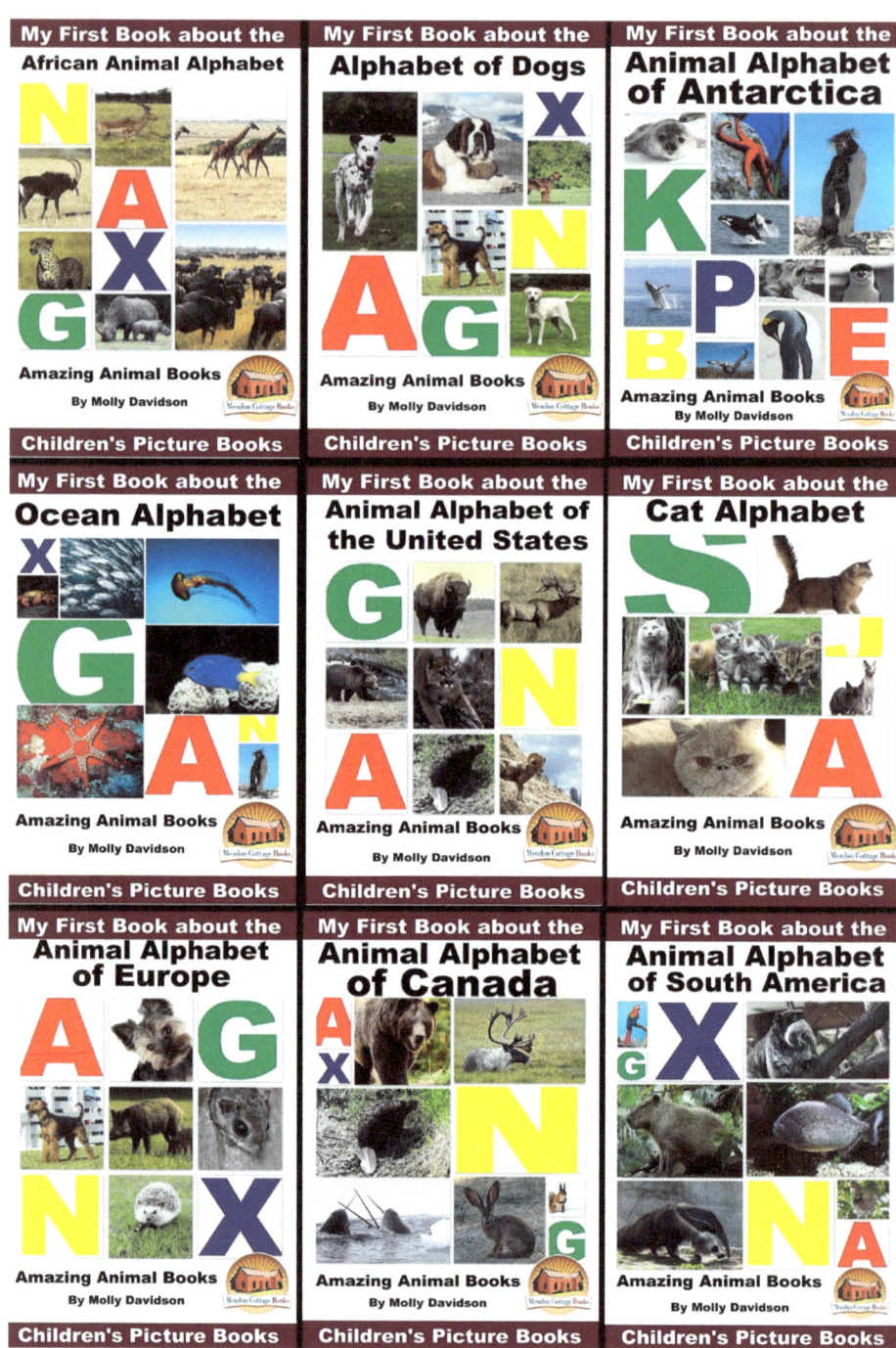

Our books are available at

1. Amazon.com

2. Barnes and Noble

3. Itunes

4. Kobo

5. Smashwords

6. Google Play Books

Download Free Books!
http://MendonCottageBooks.com

Publisher

JD-Biz Corp

P O Box 374

Mendon, Utah 84325

http://www.jd-biz.com/

www.ingramcontent.com/pod-product-compliance
Lightning Source LLC
Chambersburg PA
CBHW050844290526
45792CB00002B/512